FOR HARRY AND ABI
With special thanks to all the cowboys and cowgirls I have met
along the trail.

Cataloguing-in-Publication data
A catalogue record for this book is available from the British Library

ISBN 1-85004-050-8

First published in 1996 by Breslich & Foss Limited,
20 Wells Mews, London W1P 3FJ

Conceived and produced by Breslich & Foss, London
*Project editor:* Janet Ravenscroft
*Designed by:* Nigel Partridge
*Additional artwork:* Anthony Duke
*Photography:* David Armstrong and George Zawadzki

Printed in Hong Kong

First edition 10 9 8 7 6 5 4 3 2 1

PICTURE CREDITS
Breslich & Foss are grateful to the following individuals and institutions for
permission to reproduce illustrations: Bob Langrish: p5, p12 (top, center),
p17 (center), p22, p23, p24 (top), p28. Breslich & Foss/High Desert Museum,
Bend, Oregon: p10 (top). Breslich & Foss/Oregon Historical Society: p10 (center).
Denver Public Library, Western History Department: p16 (bottom right),
p20 (bottom), p24 (bottom), p25. Dover Publications: p13 (bottom).
Peter Newark's Western Americana: p1, p2, p6 (top), p7, p8, p9, p10, p12
(bottom), p13 (top), p14, p15, p16 (top, center, bottom left), p17 (top), p18, p19,
p24 (center), p26 (bottom left, right), p27 (top right, bottom left, bottom right).
Range/Bettmann: p3, p20 (top), p26 (center),
p27 (top left). Texas State Library, Archives Division: p6 (center).

Jacket foreground *Mounting a Wild One* by Frederic Remington,
Range/Bettmann; background *Cowboys Roping a Steer* by C.M. Russell, Peter
Newark's Western Americana.
Endpapers: *American cowboys* by unknown photographer, Range/Bettmann.

# THE
# COWBOY'S
# HANDBOOK

★ ★ ★ ★ ★

*How to Become a Hero of
the Wild West*

TOD CODY

# COWBOY GEAR

A cowboy's clothes and equipment had to be hard-wearing. There was no room for luggage on the trail drive and most cowboys wore the same things for months. Mud-caked and smelly, these clothes were often burned at the end of the journey.

### CLOTHES FOR COWBOYS

Cowboys didn't like to wear coats because they got in the way of roping. They preferred sleeveless leather jackets ("vests") with deep pockets that could hold money, a tobacco pouch, matches, and a tally book and pencil. In this book, cowboys kept a count of the herd and any stray animals. In case of bad weather, a long oilskin raincoat called a "slicker" was kept rolled and tied to the back of the saddle.

Cowboys would spend two or three months' pay on custom-made boots. Pointed toes let the boots slide easily into the stirrup and slip free if the cowboy was thrown from his horse.

Some cowboys liked to wear spurs fitted with heel chains and pear-shaped metal pieces called "jinglebobs" which made a light jingling sound that soothed the cattle. Spurs were not used to punish a horse but to guide his speed and direction.

## THE COWBOY'S HAT

The best-known hat was the Stetson, which cowboys called the "John B" after its maker, The John B Stetson Company. Early Texas cowboys favored high-crown hats like the Sugar Loaf Sombrero, whose wide brim served as a sunshade and an umbrella. The low-crowned Plainsman and the Montana Peak were ideal for windy regions. A cowboy's hat sometimes served as a water bucket!

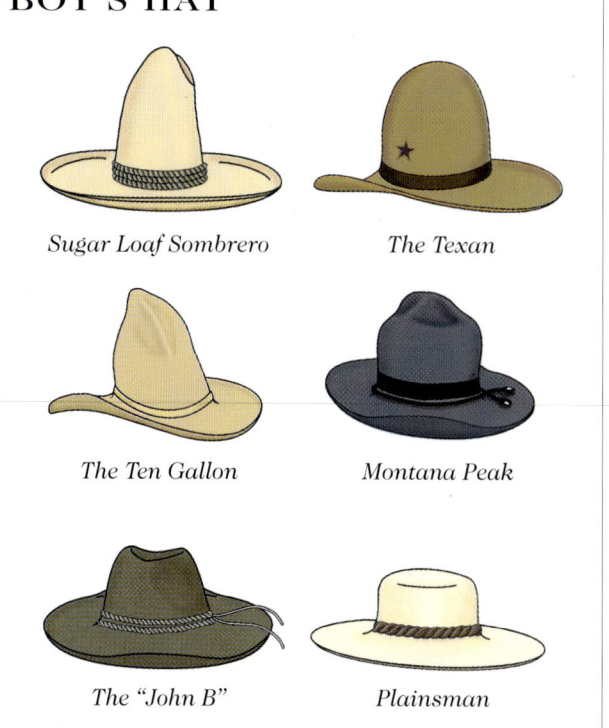

*Sugar Loaf Sombrero*

*The Texan*

*The Ten Gallon*

*Montana Peak*

*The "John B"*

*Plainsman*

# READY TO HIT THE TRAIL!

*What to wear when you're riding the range*

## HAT

You can use it to signal to other cowboys, beat trail dust off your clothes and to hold food for your horse. A true cowboy wears his hat when he's sleeping.

## SHIRT

Cowboy shirts are usually made of heavy flannel cloth – ideal because it is hard-wearing, doesn't show the dirt, and soaks up sweat.

## PANTS

Cowboys originally refused to wear jeans because they were worn by miners and farm laborers. Pants (trousers) made of thick woolen material are more comfortable to wear on horseback.

## CHAPS

These thick leather leg-coverings will protect your legs from cow horns, rope burns, scrapes and scratches. They also give a better grip to the saddle.

## BOOTS

The pointed toes and high heels are designed for riding, not for walking. That's why cowboys in the movies walk the way they do!

## BANDANNA

Soak it in water, roll it up into a wad and place it under your hat to keep cool during a hot spell. You can also use it to filter muddy water and blindfold a "spooked" horse.

## LONG JOHNS

Cowboys like to wear red flannel all-in-ones called long johns. These have a trapdoor button flap in the seat of the pants for convenience.

# MAKING CHAPS

These "batwing" chaps (pronounced "shaps") will protect your legs from scratches.

WHAT YOU WILL NEED:
★ *two rectangles of material that reach from your ankles to about 12½ cm (5 in) above your waist and that wrap loosely around your legs*
★ *tape measure*
★ *pencil*
★ *scissors (TAKE CARE)*
★ *masking tape*
★ *felt for "conchas" and decorations*
★ *8 shoelaces*

1 Measure your inside leg and mark this down one long edge of the material. Draw a wide are from a few inches above your waist to your crotch. Draw a curved shape down the outside leg. Cut it out. Make a second leg the opposite shape.

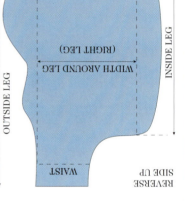

2 Bend the waistband over where your belt will go and tape down. Make holes front and back for the laces that hold the leg together. Cut out circles of felt to make 8 "conchas."

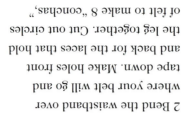

Chaps are usually made from leather, but imitation leather or any heavy no-fray material will do.

To make your chaps even fancier, glue a felt fringe down the edges.

Decorate the chaps with traditional cowboy designs such as a cactus, a horseshoe, or a five-pointed star (see page 17) made from felt or scraps of material.

3 Turn the material the right way round and thread your belt through the waistband. To fasten the chaps around your legs, take the material around to meet at the sides, thread the laces through the back and make a knot.

then make holes through them. Thread laces through the conchas and the front of the material and knot them so they don't slip out.

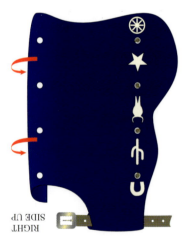

**BLANKET**
A short blanket placed under the saddle prevents the horse from getting a sore or chafed back.

**STIRRUPS**
The stirrups are set for "long-legged" riding so the cowboy can stand up if the riding gets rough.

**FENDER**
Fenders protect the rider's legs from the horse's sweat.

**SADDLE HORN**
When lassoing an animal from horseback, the cowboy wraps or "dallies," one end of his rope around the horn to stop it slipping.

**CANTLE**
The raised cantle helps the cowboy stay in the saddle.

**"Shotguns" and "Woolies"**

Mexican *vaqueros* protected their legs from the thorny brush by wearing *chaparejos* which cowboys shortened to "chaps." "Shotguns" were tube-shaped and looked like a double-barreled shotgun; "woolies" were made from curly Angora goat skin. Cowboys liked "batwings" because they could wrap them around their legs without removing their boots.

**Cracking the Whip**

Most cowboys used a short whip called a quirt made from braided strips of rawhide and attached to a wristband. A long, coiled bullwhip was used to drive animals out of thick brush. These whips were used in the days of the pioneers by "bull whackers" to "sting" teams of oxen into action. A practiced bull whacker could lift a fly off a bullock's ear from 10 ft (3 m) away. Australian cattle drovers have the best whips in the world because they are made from kangaroo hide.

**In the Saddle**

The saddle was the cowboy's most important piece of equipment because without it he couldn't work. The horse he rode would belong to the rancher who employed him, but the saddle was his own and it had to be the best he could afford. It also had to be comfortable because he would be in it from sunrise to sunset for months on end. A good saddle could last a cowboy his working life.

# ON THE TRAIL

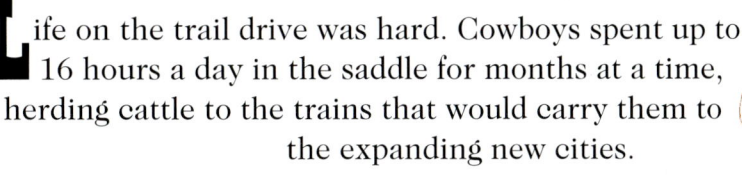

Life on the trail drive was hard. Cowboys spent up to 16 hours a day in the saddle for months at a time, herding cattle to the trains that would carry them to the expanding new cities.

## GOING NORTH

During the Civil War (1861–65), when the men were away fighting, longhorn cattle roamed free on the plains of midwest America and multiplied in great numbers. After the war the North was hungry for beef and the South had plenty of cattle so cowboys were employed to

*Herding cattle across a stream*

drive the animals from Texas to Abilene and Dodge City in Kansas where the railheads (terminals) were.

## THE TRAIL DRIVE CREW

The trail boss had to have a good knowledge of the country, be an excellent tracker, and be able to make sign with Indians. The point riders kept the leading cattle in a point or arrowhead shape and kept them moving in the right direction. The swing riders moved along with the herd and made sure the cattle did not spread out too far. The flank riders would watch out for strays and bring them into line. The drag riders, or tailers, had the worst job of all, riding for hours through thick clouds of choking dust. They moved along the stragglers at the rear of the herd and protected them

## COWBOY WISDOM

Not many cowboys went to school but they were often clever and had a lively way of speaking. Here are a few traditional cowboy sayings:

☞ "Never get up before breakfast. If you have to get up before breakfast, eat breakfast first."

☞ "The quickest way to double your money is to fold it over and put it back in your pocket."

☞ "If someone out-draws you, smile and walk away. There's plenty of time to look tough when you're out of sight."

☞ "Admire a big horse, saddle a small one."

☞ "There's a lot more to riding a horse than just sitting in the saddle and letting your feet hang down."

☞ "When in doubt, let your horse do the thinking."

from being picked off by cattle thieves or "rustlers." The cook, known as "Cookie," would drive the chuck wagon and move on ahead of the herd if the trail was well known. If not, he would drive up alongside them, followed by the wrangler, the cowboy in charge of the spare horses that were kept in a group of up to a hundred strong called the *remuda*.

Cowboys known as cowpunchers would travel with the cattle on the trains, prodding or punching them with poles to save weak and helpless animals from being crushed. The cattle would be slaughtered and refrigerated at the end of the line in Chicago. A few cowboys volunteered to drive the horses and wagons back along the trail to the ranch. Other cowboys vowed never to return.

*Cowboys rope a runaway steer*

## COWBOY RAPS!

To pass the time, cowboys liked to make up poems that were spoken with a beat like a modern rap. The first three lines rhymed and the last ended with a joke. Here's a verse from "Life Gets Tedious, Don't It!":

There's a dormouse chawing on the pantry
door,
He's been at it for a month or more,
When he gets through he'll sure be sore,
'Cos there ain't a darn thing in there!

Now make up your own cowboy rap.

# Diary of a Trail Driver

## MONDAY

We've been on the trail for a month now. We've done 200 miles and there's another 400 miles to go. We need to get the cattle across these bluffs before sunset. It's too dangerous to be down here. The place is crawling with rattlesnakes. The sun is beating down and the cattle are hot and thirsty. It's hard work keeping them moving. I'm hot and sticky myself, but I'm sucking on a bullet to quench my thirst. I can't wait until we reach the mountains so I can fill up my Stetson and drink the cool, clear water from the springs.

## TUESDAY

Breakfast was the same as last night's supper — sourdough bread, pork and beans and strong black coffee. Today we had to cross the

Brazos River. Getting 1,500 head of cattle across the water ain't no mean feat. Even a fish popping out of the water can spook them.

## WEDNESDAY

Mexican Bob is coughing badly so Cookie brewed him his cure-all mixture. All of us, man and beast, are tired and edgy today. Last night, when it was my night watch guarding the cattle, I had to rub tobacco juice in my eyes to stop them from closing. It's known as a "rouser" and it smarts like heck, but it sure does the trick.

## THURSDAY

Reached the mountains at last! There's spring water aplenty, but the going is still tricky. It's Cookie's birthday today, and he came up with half a jug of whiskey at the campfire tonight, and we had a good old singsong. Even so, I can't relax. There's a feeling in the air that I don't like. 'Reckon there's a storm coming.

## FRIDAY

At about 3 a.m. we could feel something building up in the air and we could see strange blue lights flickering around the horns of the herd. This is St Elmo's Fire, a sure warning of a storm. Suddenly, there was a blinding flash of lightning followed by an almighty crack of thunder. The herd spooked and started up. We leapt on our horses because we knew what was coming: stampede! Our only hope was to follow the herd, head them off and circle them as best we could. We had to keep our wits about us though. If you fall off your horse in front of a stampeding herd, you'll be trampled into a mess of blood 'n' bone in seconds flat. It took us three hard hours of riding to bring them round and we lost 20 head of cattle.

## SATURDAY

Made sign with some Comanches for half an hour and let them have a gimpy steer or two. Cookie traded a pork belly for some trinkets.

## SUNDAY

Talked about what we'll do when we reach Dodge City. I'm gonna have a long hot bath, a shave and a haircut, change these filthy old clothes and then hit the town. Last time I blew all my wages in just three days but it was worth it. Here's to the next time!

## BRANDING

The long trail drives north took place in the fall. Winter provided little work or wages for cowboys, but spring was the time for busting wild mustangs, training new horses, and for rounding up the cattle in order to brand the rumps and notch the ears of new calves.

Each ranch had its own mark and registered it in a pocket-sized brand book produced by the local cattlemen's association. Trail bosses carried a copy to help identify stray brands. Out on the open ranges cattle from different ranches would graze together so roundups were organized to "cut out" and return stray steers to their rightful owners. Yearling calves would be "chopped out" and dragged to the branding fire. Branding was a frightening and painful experience for a calf. An unbranded animal is called a maverick, thanks to one Colonel Maverick who decided to identify his cattle by not branding them at all – he lost a lot of animals that way.

Some cowboys knew what it felt like to be branded. The quickest way for a cowboy to seal deep cuts was to apply the red-hot blade of a knife or branding iron to the wound!

## RUSTLERS

Branding didn't stop the cattle thieves. These "rustlers" would catch a calf and change the owner's brand to their own by using "running irons." A rustler would need two or three running irons, one in the shape of a circle, one a zig-zag, and one an L shape. With these he could alter just about any branding mark to his own.

*An experienced cowboy*

## MAKING A BRAND

Letters, numbers, geometric symbols, and little pictures were all used by ranchers to identify their animals. Design your own personal brand to sign your letters. You can make two patterns with just one potato.

WHAT YOU WILL NEED:
★ *potato*
★ *knife (TAKE CARE)*
★ *paintbrush*
★ *poster paints*
★ *paper*

1 Cut the potato in half. Trace the shape you want with the end of the knife, then cut away the area around your design to a depth of about 1 cm or ½ inch.

2 Use a paintbrush to apply a thin layer of paint to the brand. Take care when pressing it to the paper so that the image doesn't smudge.

# THE CHUCK WAGON

**O**ut on the range, the chuck wagon was where cowboys could find hot food and dry clothes, and before bedding down for the night they could gather around the campfire to swap songs and stories. Cowboys who snored were sent downwind of the wagon.

## HOME ON THE RANGE

The chuck wagon carried the food supplies for a three- to four-month trail drive and served as a barber's shop, dentist's, doctor's surgery and general store. The person in charge of the wagon was usually known as "Cookie."

After the trail boss, Cookie was the most important member of the crew. He was often an older cowboy who would have learned by trial and error how to make tasty meals from basic foodstuffs.

..............................
*A chuck wagon*

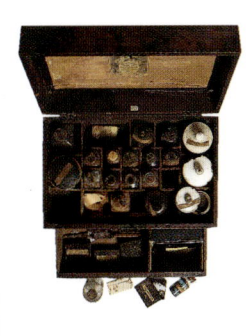

## COOKIE'S CURES

On the trail drive the nearest doctor could be over 200 miles away, so doctoring would fall upon Cookie. Match the ailments with the remedies and discover whether you've got what it takes to become camp doctor.

PROBLEM:
1 Aches and pains
2 Bad cough
3 Broken leg
4 Earache
5 Fever
6 Gangrenous wounds
7 Snake bite

TREATMENT:
A Cover brown paper with mustard and strap it to your chest.
B Cut the snake's head off, boil it in water, and drink the soup.
C Rub on horse liniment and axle grease.
D Drink a mixture of horse liniment, water and whiskey, place onion skins on your feet, and rest facing north.
E Make a splint by pushing a rifle down your boot and tying it tightly to your leg.
F Apply kerosene and tobacco juice to the wounds and bandage.
G Place a piece of old pork in your ear.

ANSWERS: 1C, 2A, 3E, 4G, 5D, 6F, 7B.

These included sowbelly (bacon), beans, eggs carefully packed in flour, lard, potatoes, salt, sugar, baking soda and sometimes dried or canned fruit. There would also be hundreds of bags of coffee. Arbuckles coffee was the favorite because each bag contained a stick of peppermint candy, and cowboys would eagerly crank the grinder and do other chores for Cookie in return for this special treat.

### WHAT'S ON THE MENU?
Cookie would be up before first light to prepare breakfast, then would ride ahead to set up the next meal for the crew. Cowboys who dared to ask what was on the menu would hear from Cookie, "It's brown, hot, and there's plenty of it!"

Dirty plates were thrown in the "wreck pan" and scoured with sand if there wasn't enough water to wash them.

## THREE-BEAN CHILI

The cowboy word for food was "chuck." When making this chuck, add the chili powder gradually – once in, you can't take it out!

WHAT YOU WILL NEED:
★ 1 clove garlic, crushed
★ 1 tablespoon vegetable oil
★ 16 oz (400 g) canned chopped tomatoes
★ 8 oz (200 g) canned red kidney beans
★ 8 oz (200 g) canned pinto beans
★ 8 oz (200 g) canned black-eyed beans
★ 2 teaspoons dried oregano
★ 1 to 3 teaspoons chili powder (Cowboys liked their chuck spicy)
★ 1 tablespoon vinegar
★ 1 vegetable stock cube, crumbled
★ salt to taste

Using a heavy pan, lightly fry the garlic in the oil over a low heat. Add the tomatoes, drained beans, oregano, chili powder, vinegar, and stock cube and bring to the boil. Take a tablespoon of the mixture, allow it to cool, then taste it. Add more chili and salt if required. Reduce the heat, cover and simmer gently for about an hour, stirring occasionally. Add water as necessary to keep the chuck liquid.

Serve with rice, corn chips, or tortillas to feed two hungry cowboys.

# ANIMALS

**N**ot all cowboys owned their own horses. When a cowboy was given a job, he would be lent a horse by the rancher. The horse and the cowboy then worked together to herd the cattle and protect them from accidents and predators.

### THE MUSTANG

Mustangs are the direct descendants of the Andalusian horses brought over to Mexico by the Spaniards in the 16th century. Some of these horses ran wild and, left to fend for themselves, they became spirited, strong and short-tempered. The Mexican cowboys (*vaqueros*) began to catch them. Once caught, they were "busted" and "broken" – tamed and trained to perform different tasks.

### THE COWBOY'S PARTNER

Cutting horses were the best-trained horses and were paired off with the most skillful riders. Their role was to cut out (separate) unbranded cattle from the rest of the herd so they could be branded. The American quarter horse was a specialist at this work.

*The American quarter horse*

*Wild mustangs*

The roping horse was a good all-rounder, able to stop dead at the right moment as soon as a lasso tightened around a bronc or steer. A bronc is a partly tamed mustang with a natural talent for bucking. Bronc busters would boastfully offer to catch a bronc to order in any color except sky-blue pink!

Circle horses were tough little cow ponies with lots of staying power that could run fast over many miles of open prairie rounding up strays or chasing mustangs.

The night horse was an old timer and not easily spooked. He and the night watch cowboy would stand guard over the resting herd. Some said old night horses could see best in the dark.

River horses were trained to swim high in deep water and low in strong currents. They seemed to sense where a river was safe to cross and could save days in finding safe cattle crossings along the trail.

### TEXAS LONGHORNS

Like mustangs, longhorn cattle were descended from animals introduced by the Spanish settlers. Longhorns were tough but quick tempered and dangerous to handle because of their sharp horns. They also provided poor quality beef, so eventually they were bred with fatter, calmer breeds such as the Aberdeen Angus imported from Britain.

*A Texas longhorn*

### WESTERN WILDLIFE

One of the cowboy's chief duties throughout the year was to protect the rancher's cattle from predators and other pests. During the harsh northern winters, grizzly bears and American timber wolves would happily make a meal of weak animals. Small burrowing squirrels called prairie dogs, and jack rabbits (a kind of hare) ate the grass that the cattle needed to graze on. A whole range of creatures caused problems for cowboys.

**SKUNK** Cowboys knew to stay well clear of skunks because of the foul-smelling liquid they sprayed when cornered. They also carried the fatal disease rabies, which they passed on in their bites.

**RATTLESNAKE** Rattlesnakes have a chunky body, wide head, and a rattle on the end of the tail that can be sounded as a warning. Rattlesnakes seeking warmth would sometimes crawl into a cowboy's bedroll or into his boots!

**GILA MONSTER** This poisonous lizard is more feared by cowboys than a rattlesnake. Its bite can be fatal because once it has bitten no amount of shaking, kicking, or beating will loosen its hold.

**SCORPION** A scorpion's sting is painful but not deadly to someone healthy. Mexican *vaqueros* believed that a horsehair lariat laid around their bedroll would ward off scorpions.

*A rattlesnake*

---

## TRACKING

Cowboys need good tracking skills to find stray cattle, hunt down predators, and keep an eye out for signs of rustlers. If you can't find tracks straightaway, walk in a large sweeping circle until you pick up a trail, then read it carefully. Fresh tracks are clear and sharp – the deeper the print, the larger the animal.

If there is water in the tracks, did it seep in through the ground or was it rain-filled? Has the imprint gone hard or is it still soft? Can you see leaves with rotting sides face up? Are there any fresh breaks in twigs or tall grasses?

Never track alone and never track dangerous animals too closely. If you come face to face with a large animal, back off very slowly, speaking or singing softly.

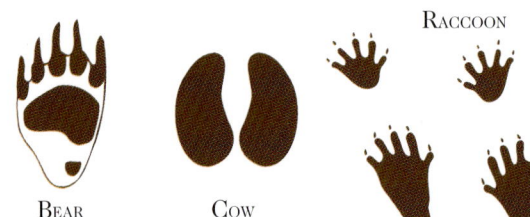

BEAR    COW    RACCOON

# COMMUNICATIONS

For centuries, Indians used smoke signals to communicate across great distances. The white men who moved west used the Pony Express and telegraph. Cowboys and Indians used sign language to trade with each other.

## COWBOYS AND INDIANS

It is a Hollywood myth that cowboys and Indians were always fighting; in fact, cowboys had far more in common with the Indians than with city folk. Trail bosses couldn't do their jobs properly if they couldn't communicate with the native people. They needed to trade and pay a toll to the Indians whose land they crossed on the drive north.

*A Pony Express rider*

## COWBOY SLANG

Cowboys have a colorful language all of their own. Learn a few of these phrases and you'll be welcome around any campfire.

☞ "I was chewing gravel."
   I was thrown from a bucking bronco.

☞ "I've had the mulligrubs all day."
   I feel sad.

☞ "It's time to get into my flea trap."
   I'm going to bed.

☞ "That's a real toad floater."
   It's raining heavily.

☞ "That horse is worth doodly squat."
   That horse is worthless.

☞ "John just stepped off the trail."
   John got married/got a job in town.

☞ "Don't hog-tie me with your fancy words!"
   Don't confuse me!

## THE PONY EXPRESS

The Pony Express ran between St Joseph, Missouri, and Sacramento in California across two thousand miles of treacherous country. Letters and packages were stuffed into a saddlebag or *mochila* and speeded across the land by a team of relay riders. It was dangerous work so "Wanted" posters were put up seeking: "Young, skinny, wiry fellows, not over 18. Must be expert riders, willing to risk death daily. Orphans preferred. Wages $25 per week."

The Pony Express ended after 18 months because the new transcontinental telegraph

*Indians used smoke signals to talk to each other*

link could transmit messages across the country in minutes instead of days.

### INDIAN MESSAGES

Indians used all kinds of natural things to communicate with each other. They would build a smoky fire from wet straw and green twigs, then wave a rug over it to spell out messages in puffs of smoke. At night, a blanket waved over a bright fire made a flash that could be seen from miles away.

A bunch of fresh grass laid on the ground would be a sign that someone had just passed that way. Two or three stones piled on top of each other might be a warning or it could indicate a direction. Finding a tomahawk painted red was a warning, and a broken arrow on the ground meant "Go no further."

## HAND SIGNALS

If cowboys didn't speak the local language, they could use signs to trade with the Indians they met along the trail.

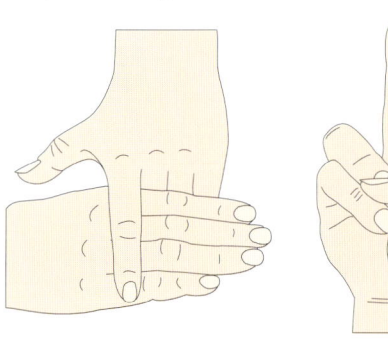

HORSE. Place your left index and middle fingers astride your right hand.

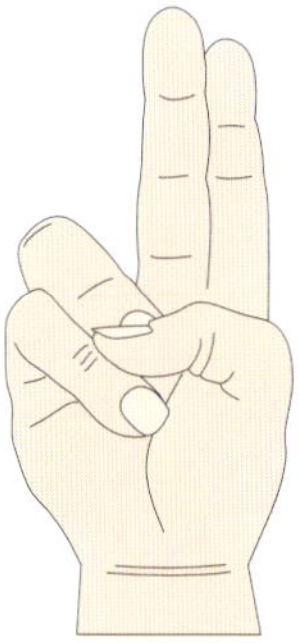

FRIEND. Raise your right hand with the index and middle finger extended.

# LAW AND ORDER

In the movies, cowboys are always getting into fights and shooting people. In fact, very few cowboys ever shot anyone. Outlaws were robbers and murderers, often with a price on their heads. Lawmen were sometimes as violent as the criminals they pursued.

*Cowboy trouble in a frontier town*

### PEACEKEEPERS

Marshal Wyatt Earp acted as a lawman in Wichita, Dodge City, and Tombstone, but he also ran gambling houses and took cuts from saloon bar takings and the saloon girls' earnings. The famous gunfight at the O.K. Corral took place in Tombstone, Arizona, in October, 1881, when the Clantons and the McLaurys faced Wyatt Earp, two of his brothers, and a dentist friend known as "Doc" Holliday. During the gunfight, three of the gang were killed within just 60 seconds. Earp lived to be 80 years old.

*Wyatt Earp*

The marshal of Abilene, Kansas, was James Butler "Wild Bill" Hickok, one of the best shots in the West. Hickok could twirl and juggle guns like a circus performer and wore his guns with handles facing forward so that he had to cross his arms when drawing to fire.

### TEXAS RANGERS

The Texas Rangers claimed they were: "Brutal to enemies, loyal to friends, courteous to women, and kind to old ladies." They were formed in 1835 to patrol the Mexican border and deal with outlaws, rustlers, and hostile Indians. The first Rangers had to provide their own horses, guns, and ammunition and carve their own "silver star" badges from Mexican one-peso coins. A Texas Ranger was expected to ride like a Mexican, track like a Comanche,

*Texas Rangers*

and shoot like a Kentuckian. There was an unwritten rule that said: One job, one Ranger, no matter how great the task. There was a similar attitude among Canada's Royal North-West Mounted Police, formed in 1873. Legend has it that Wyatt Earp said of the Mounties: "If I'd have had one of those red-coated fellas backing me up, I'd have cleared up Tombstone for sure."

*The working cowboy's gun*

## WINNING WEAPONS

The Colt .45 Peacemaker was the favorite gun of both lawmen and outlaws. They liked its short 4¾ inch (12 cm) barrel because it made the gun easier to handle in a quick draw. The

*Colt .45 Peacemaker*

accuracy of a handgun was usually around a distance of 50 paces.

Working cowboys preferred the Colt Frontier six-shooter with a 7½ inch (19 cm) barrel. It was designed by Samuel Colt and took the same ammunition as the Winchester 1873 Model repeating rifle .44 caliber, also known as "the gun that won the West" because it was powerful and accurate.

Cowboys seldom wore their guns when riding because they were so bulky. There was also the danger that they might accidentally go off. Instead, they would be kept in the saddlebag or carried in the chuck wagon along with the rifles and the rest of the kit.

## MAKING A SHERIFF'S BADGE

Once you know how to make a traditional five-pointed Texas star, you can use it to decorate all kinds of cowboy gear. Here's how to make a sheriff's badge of office.

WHAT YOU WILL NEED:
★ *a mug to draw around to make a big circle*
★ *string*
★ *pencil*
★ *cardboard*
★ *ruler*
★ *craft knife (TAKE CARE)*
★ *aluminum foil*
★ *tape*
★ *safety pin*

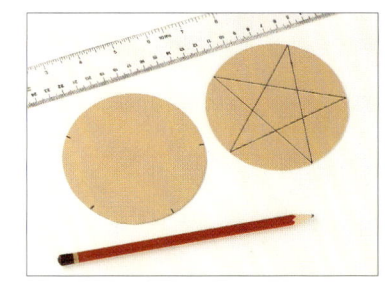

1 Measure the circumference of the mug with a piece of string and divide the number by five. Cut out the circle and mark the five points. Join them up.

2 Cut out the star and cover it with foil. Write your name on top with a pencil, taking care not to pierce the foil. Tape a

safety pin to the back of the badge so you can wear it.

**Billy the Kid**

When Billy the Kid was shot dead at the age of 21 it was said that he had already killed 21 people. He was only tried and convicted for killing one man, and that was Sheriff Brady of Lincoln County. Billy was sent to prison for this murder but, although his hands and feet were manacled together, he managed to shoot two armed deputies and escape. Three months later Pat Garrett, the new sheriff of Lincoln County and an old friend of Billy, tracked him down and shot him twice in the back.

Newspapers spread Billy the Kid's reputation as a ruthless killer and accidentally began the legend of the "left-handed gun" by printing his photograph in reverse, so that it looked as if he was left-handed.

**Belle Starr**

Belle Starr fought in the American Civil War dressed as a man. After the war she took to dealing cards in saloons and singing in dance halls before turning to crime. With her husband Sam and her gang, she rustled cattle, robbed stores and ranches, and ran illegal whiskey to an Indian reservation. When a deputy sheriff was shot by a woman in men's clothing, the lawmen came looking for Belle. She let down her hair, put rouge on her cheeks and wore fancy frills and petticoats, and because she looked nothing like the assassin, the charges were dropped. But it wasn't long before a $10,000 reward was offered for Belle and her husband and in 1889 Belle Starr, queen of the outlaws, was found dead on the trail, shot in the back by an unknown bandit.

**Black Bart**

Black Bart began robbing stagecoaches in his sixties after retiring from farming and mining. He was charming and well-educated and he left a poem at the scene of each of his crimes. He always carried a rifle that he pointed at the stage driver but never fired, and spoke the same four words at a robbery: "Throw down the box." He wore a long white coat and a flour sack with eye holes cut out of it to cover his head. There was no real clue to his identity until he held up a Wells Fargo stagecoach from Sonora. On breaking open the strong box to get at the money, Bart cut his hand and wrapped the wound with his handkerchief. Without time to write a poem, he made his escape with over $4,000. Somewhere along the trail he threw away the blood-soaked handkerchief. On it was a tell-tale laundry mark – "F.O.X.7." Thanks to this, Wells Fargo detectives tracked down their quarry to a San Francisco hotel where they arrested an elegant, well-spoken old gentleman, one Charles E. Bolton Esq., alias Black Bart!

**The Wild Bunch**

Butch Cassidy and the Sundance Kid were highly professional thieves who preferred robbing trains to stagecoaches. During their careers they stole thousands

*Billy might not have been left-handed at all*

REWARD ($5,000.00)
Reward for the capture, dead or alive, of one Wm. Wright, better known as "BILLY THE KID"
Age, 18. Height, 5 feet, 3 inches. Weight, 125 lbs. Light hair, grey eyes and even features. He is the leader of the worst band of desperadoes the Territory has ever had to deal with. The above reward will be paid for his capture or positive proof of his death.
JIM DALTON

REWARD $10,000 IN GOLD COIN
DEAD OR ALIVE
of
SAM and BELLE STARR
Wanted for Robbery, Murder, Treason and other acts against the peace and dignity of the U.S.
Will be paid by the U.S. Government for the apprehension
THOMAS CRAIL, Major, 8th Missouri County, Commanding

## CALAMITY JANE

Martha Jane Cannary liked to dress as a man, barge into saloons, drink too much, get into arguments and break things, which is how she got her nickname Calamity Jane. She claimed to have served as an army scout, Indian fighter, and wagon driver, but despite being a sharpshooter she never shot anybody. She became famous because she dressed and acted like a man in the days when women were supposed to be "ladylike." Jane was a friend of Wild Bill Hickok and traveled with him in Buffalo Bill's Wild West show. When interviewed at Hickok's grave in 1900, she said that when she died she wanted to be buried beside him. Three years later she was.

*Martha "Calamity Jane" Cannary was no villain, but her behavior scandalized a lot of people.*

of dollars from railroad companies. They were so successful with the Wild Bunch and the Hole-in-the-Wall gangs that Union Pacific, whose trains they often attacked, put together a team of men to hunt them down. Some people say that Butch and Sundance were eventually shot dead in Bolivia, others claim that they survived for many years. The truth remains a mystery.

*The Hole-in-the-Wall gang looking more like bankers than robbers: standing (left to right) William Carver and Harvey Logan; seated (left to right) Sundance Kid, Ben Kilpatrick, and Butch Cassidy*

# COWBOY SKILLS

Cowboys learned roping and riding from the *vaqueros* who first brought cattle to Texas from Mexico in the 18th century. Cowboys liked to show off their skills for the fun of it and so rodeos began.

## THE ROPE

The braided rawhide leather rope the *vaquero* used was called *la reata* and this was changed by the cowboy into "lariat." The lariat's main use was for lassoing, but it was also used to drag firewood, to haul out wagons stuck in the mud, and to build makeshift corrals.

Roping was the most difficult thing a cowboy had to learn, but every cowboy had to be skilled with his lariat so that he could go about his daily business. A lariat could be anywhere between 30 and 60 ft (9 and 18 m) long, depending on the job for which it was needed.

## THE RODEO

The word rodeo comes from the Spanish word *rodear* meaning to encircle or round up. Probably the best-known rodeo in the world today is the annual Calgary Stampede which takes place in Alberta, Canada. There are five main events in rodeos: saddle bronc riding, bareback bronc riding, steer wrestling, calf roping, and bull riding.

*Cowboys still use lariats to lasso calves*

# ROPE SPINNING AND LASSOING

Any cowboy will tell you that it takes a lot of practice to handle a rope well, so if you don't succeed the first time, keep trying! Use braided rope or all-purpose rope from hardware stores, or cowboy rope from Western or equestrian stores.

**WHAT YOU WILL NEED FOR ROPE SPINNING:**
★ 2 m (7 ft) rope, 13 mm (½ in) in diameter
★ adhesive tape
★ marker pen

1 Measure 15 cm (6 in) from one end of rope, double it over and tape to make an "eye" just big enough for rope to pass through. Thread rope through eye to make a loop, and tie the knot in end of rope. Measure 51 cm (20 in) from knot, and mark this on rope. Pull rope along loop up to marker. Hold knot in upturned right hand and let loop rest on hooked first finger. The eye now hangs down on your right. Your left hand supports loop, palm down, at waist level.

2 Lean forward with right arm outstretched. Turn right hand over so that rope falls between finger and thumb, and drop the loop spinning it from the wrist in a counter-clockwise movement.

**WHAT YOU WILL NEED FOR LASSOING:**
★ 5 m (16 ft) rope, 13 mm (½ in) in diameter (Stiff rope works best)
★ adhesive tape
★ marker pen

1 Tape a large "eye" at one end of rope. Make a mark on the rope 2 m (7 ft) from eye. Thread other end of rope through eye, and pull rope along to the marker to make a big loop. Grip loop and rope in your right hand about 51 cm (20 in) from eye. Hold end of rope and spare coils in left hand.

2 With right arm outstretched, swing loop above your head in a smooth, counter-clockwise circle.

3 As loop comes round, let go. Let go of coils in left hand, but keep hold of end of rope. Practice lassoing outdoors, using a chair as your target.

## BRONC RIDING

Working cowboys rounded up wild mustangs and a "bronc buster" would be employed at $5 a horse to "bust" or break the horses' wild spirits so they could be trained. A couple of "buckeroos" (assistants) held on to the tethered horse while a bridle was slipped over its head, a saddle placed on its back, and a blindfold placed over its head. When the bronc buster had mounted the horse, the blindfold was removed, and the animal bucked wildly until it gave in and trotted obediently round the corral.

At the rodeo, saddle bronc riding shows the rider's style and skill. The rider doesn't have to be very strong, but he does need a combination of balance and rhythm to stay on his bucking bronc until the hooter sounds.

Bareback bronc riding is even harder because the rider has no reins or stirrups, just a narrow saddle-strap rigging fastened around the horse's belly. This rigging has a fixed handhold for the rider to grip with one gloved hand.

## STEER WRESTLING

In steer wrestling or "bull dogging" two cowboys pair up to pull a steer (a bullock) to the ground. Two horses are used; the steer wrestler or "dogger" is on one, the "hazer" on the other. Doggers are heavier built and usually taller than other rodeo stars because weight and strength are important in this event. The hazer keeps the steer running in a straight line. The wrestler must grasp the horns of the steer as it runs from the chute and, slipping out of the saddle, bring the steer down to the ground by wrestling its head over. He must then hold it until the signal is given to release it. The key to winning is being able to make a split-second decision on when to jump on the steer. The wrestler has to throw it over without getting his feet caught in the stirrups, and possibly breaking an ankle.

## CALF ROPING

In calf roping the rider ropes and catches a calf, throws it down and ties three of its legs together. Cowboys still catch calves this way for branding but many rodeo riders have never worked on a ranch. Now there are rodeo schools to teach riders cowboy skills.

## BULL RIDING

In this very dangerous event, the rider has to stay on an angry bull for eight seconds, holding on to a loose rope wrapped around the animal's belly. Timing when to get

*A bronc tries to unseat its rider*

The horse and rider have to work closely together in barrel racing, displaying the same skills used to "cut" (separate) calves from a herd

rodeo riders owe their lives to the quick actions of the clown.

Bull riding is the most dangerous event

off is also very important – the rider has to propel himself off the bull as it is bucking and escape from the arena while the rodeo clown distracts the animal. A bull will try to trample and gore anything that moves and many

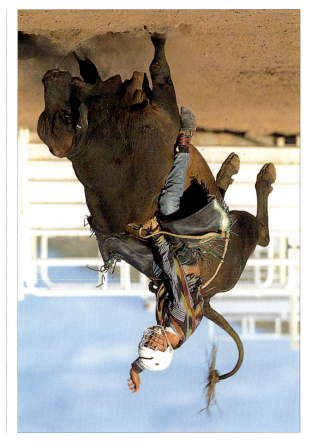

## BARREL RACING

In barrel racing, riders must race around three spaced barrels as fast as they can, and seconds are added for touching the barrels. Women compete in barrel racing because the competition is judged on horseback riding skills, not strength.

Cowgirls have competed in rodeos since 1904. The first female rodeo star was "Let Loose Lucy" Mulhall. It is said that Lucy could lasso eight galloping horses in one throw of the rope! Nowadays, all-women rodeos are very popular.

# RECREATION

On the trail or at the ranch cowboys relaxed after a hard day's riding by swapping tall stories, making things, playing cards, and singing. Once they hit town, they could go to saloons and have a good time.

## Cowboy Concerts

Campfire songs were usually accompanied by a guitar or harmonica, but at the bunkhouse cowboys could make other instruments. A rhythm section might include a washboard, pots and pans, and two large spoons. An old piece of lariat stretched from one corner of a wooden box to the top of a broom handle made a passable bass and someone blowing into a large whiskey jug made a sound like a bassoon. When it came to dancing, one or two cowboys would be "heifer" branded, which meant that they put on an apron or tied a bandanna over their heads and took the lady's part. Polkas and waltzes were the favorites.

Cowboys sometimes got into fights in saloons

Singing around the campfire

## CAMPFIRE SONGS

In the evenings cowboys liked to listen to sad songs about the loneliness and hardships they faced. All cowboys knew lullabies that they sang to soothe the herd at night. This night herding song is sung to motherless calves or "dogies."

Oh, say, little dogies, when you goin' to lay down
And give up this shiftin' and roving around?
My horse is leg-weary and I'm awful tired,
But if you get away, I am sure to be fired.
Lay down, little dogies, lay down.
Hi-yee-o, hi-yee-o, hi-yee-o.

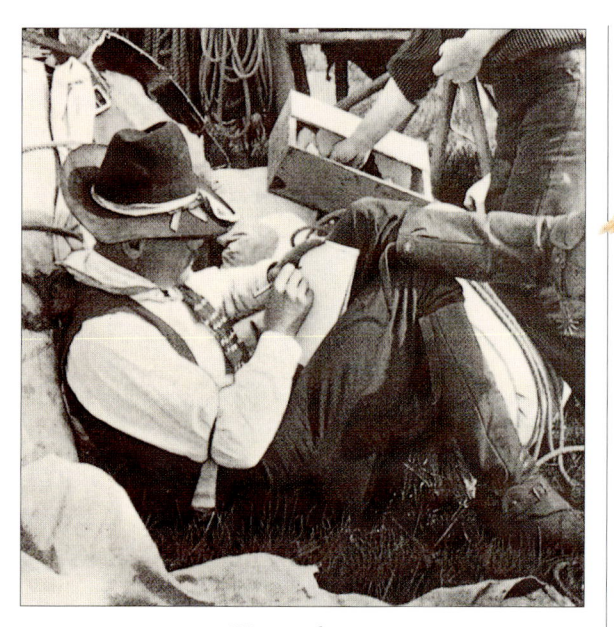

*Writing home*

### GAMES AND PASTIMES

In winter, cowboys could be holed up in a bunkhouse for weeks, so they came up with lots of ways to pass the time. They were very competitive and would bet on anything, even on which fly would fly off a side of meat first! Apart from horseshoe throwing, target shooting, knife throwing, whip cracking and roping, they might compete in spitting contests, cigarette rolling competitions, arm wrestling and "pick-a-back" in which cowboys paired up, one riding on the other's back, and tried to pull the other team's rider off his mount.

Alongside checkers, dominoes, poker and craps, cowboys played children's games like marbles and penny at the wall. In this game, coins were thrown as close to a wall as possible without touching it. To play duck on a rock, cowboys had to knock a small rock off a large one with pebbles from 20 paces away.

Horse races, trick riding, and steer wrestling were popular and they developed into rodeos.

## COWBOY BRAIDING

Cowboys were good with their hands and enjoyed drawing, wood carving, metalwork, even embroidery, crocheting, and knitting! They were probably best at leatherwork and liked to braid quirts, bridles, hat bands, and buddy bracelets.

WHAT YOU WILL NEED:
★ *3 embroidery threads, leather or cotton shoelaces, or strands of yarn, 30 cm (12 in) long*
★ *a thumb tack and a piece of board, or a safety pin*

Knot the three strands together at the top. To keep the threads taut, push the thumb tack through the knot and into the board or use a safety pin to attach the knot to a cushion that you hold between your knees.

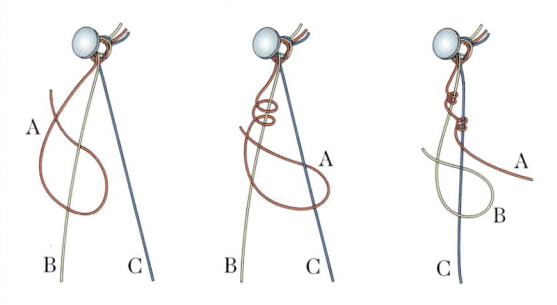

Start with strand A on the left, strand B in the middle and strand C on the right. Knot A twice around B, pushing the loop knots to the top each time, then twice around C. Leave A on your right. Knot B twice around C, then twice around A. Leave B on your right. Knot C twice around A, then twice around B. Leave C on your right. Repeat until the threads run out. Begin with three threads, then use six, working in the same way from left to right, to make a thicker band.

# BUFFALO BILL'S WILD WEST

William Frederick "Buffalo Bill" Cody was never a cowboy but he was a buffalo hunter, Pony Express rider, army scout, and cavalry soldier before starting the show he called "The Wild West" in 1882. It was a thrilling spectacle of battle re-enactments, cowboy skills and the daring pursuit of the Deadwood stage. All the tricks were performed by cowboys and Indians, including Sitting Bull. In 1891, a new "Congress of Rough Riders of the World" was added, which featured Mexican *vaqueros* and Cossacks. A popular star of the Wild West show was Annie Oakley, who was billed as

"Little Miss Sure Shot." Annie started shooting a rifle at the age of nine and as a teenager she won a national shooting championship. Annie could cut a playing card in two at 30 paces. For some of her near-impossible tricks she made special bullets that held sand and beeswax that spread as thousands of tiny pellets, making it easier to hit flying targets. However, she was still one of the best shots in the world.

*Buffalo Bill's show helped create the modern image of the cowboy*

## SALOONS

At the height of the summer cattle season, three or four hundred cowboys a day would arrive in cow towns like Abilene and Dodge City, all eager to have a good time and spend their money at the end of a hard trail drive. Saloons tried to outdo each other to attract the most customers. No expense was spared on long mahogany bars with brass rails to rest boots on, brass spittoons to catch the spittle of show-off cowboys, fancy wallpaper, crystal chandeliers, etched glass and mirrors, plush velvet drapes, pianos, pianolas, gaming tables and all manner of fancy furnishings, specially imported from the East. Cowboys would scrub off the dirt of the trail and dress up in their best "duds" (clothes) before entering these "pleasure palaces."

# COWBOYS IN THE MOVIES

In early Westerns, good guys were clean shaven and wore fancy outfits and white hats. Bad guys were scruffy, unshaven, and wore dull or black outfits and black hats.

## WESTERN HEROES

Westerns were first made in the early 1900s. Cowboys who found it hard to find jobs on the range were suddenly in demand in the new movie industry. Instead of earning $5 a day for riding and staying on wild horses, the studios paid them $25 a day just to fall off! Cowboys provided rip-roaring action sequences galloping across the plains and became the first screen stunt men.

*Roy Rogers*

The first cowboy heros were acrobatic action men like "Bronco Billy" Anderson and Tom Mix, a former Wild West show performer who thrilled audiences with his daring stunts. When sound was added to films, romantic singing cowboys like Roy Rogers and Gene Autry became popular. Later, John Wayne played strong, dependable heroes and Clint Eastwood the mysterious stranger.

## SCREEN TRICKS

In early films, if a cowboy wasn't very fast with his gun, the director would position him so that his gun hand and holster were away from the camera. The hero would then be able to hold his gun out of the holster. When the time came for the gun fight, he would simply extend his arm and it would look like a lightning-fast draw. This is why you often saw the hero standing on the right-hand side of the screen, left side on!

*Clint Eastwood*

*John Wayne*

# COWBOYS TODAY

**O**n the ranges of the modern ranch, cowboys and cowgirls need to be skilled in roping and branding, able to drive a pickup truck and tractor, and sometimes to fly a plane to spot strays.

### THE COWGIRL

The cowgirl today works on equal terms with the men and shares the same skills and duties. Like them, she will probably have college qualifications in agriculture, farming, animal husbandry, and stock-breeding. She may also enjoy demonstrating her Wild West skills and compete in professional rodeos.

### DUDE RANCHES

The first dude ranches opened their doors to paying guests over a hundred years ago. Since then, people from around the world have enjoyed pretending to be cowboys, performing cowboy chores, and taking part in roundups and brandings out West.

Theodore Roosevelt (who became the 26th president of the United States) is perhaps the

*Riding in Colorado*

*Cowboys with a mustang*

best-known "dude cowboy." As a young, rich New Yorker, "Teddy" bought a share in a western ranch and lived the life of a cowboy. He prided himself on his western knowledge, wrote articles about cowboys, and helped to promote the image of the cowboy as a man of honor.

# Code of the West

Cowboys had a code of honor that they stuck to through thick and thin. Trail bosses and cattle barons would trade thousands of cattle on the strength of a handshake and a promise to pay and deliver.

## Rule 1
A cowboy seldom says please and sorry, but he always feels much obliged for a favor and will thank you kindly.

## Rule 2
A cowboy never talks ugly in front of ladies and always tips his hat.

## Rule 3
When riding up to a ranch or homestead a cowboy shouts out, "Hello the house" to make his presence known. He will stay on his horse until invited to dismount.

## Rule 4
Before entering a homestead a cowboy unbuckles his gunbelt and removes his spurs.

## Rule 5
If a cowboy sees a stranger on the trail he rides straight toward him and says "Howdy." Veering off the trail looks suspicious.

## Rule 6
A cowboy never asks another cowboy about his past.

## Rule 7
A cowboy will risk his life to save his partner.

## Rule 8
Cowboys will be punished for bad behavior by doing all the dirty jobs or by paying a fine.

10-040-669

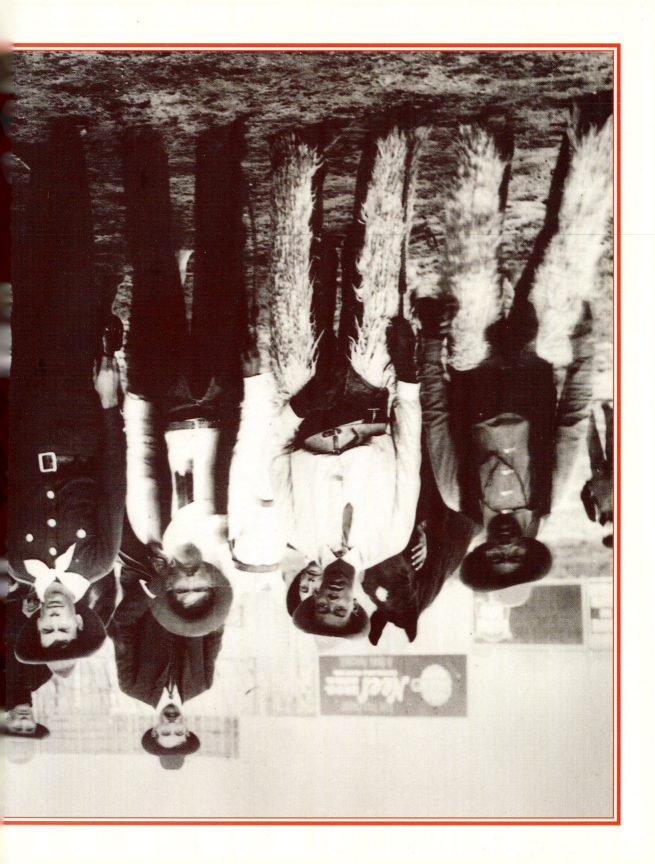